JESUS

REVOLUTION
BIBLE STUDY

How God Can Transform a Generation

Greg Laurie

Lifeway Press®
Nashville, Tennessee

EDITORIAL TEAM

Jeremy Maxfield
Writer

Joel Polk
Editorial Team Leader

Reid Patton
Content Editor

Brian Daniel
Publisher & Manager, Adult Discipleship

Susan Hill
Production Editor

Brandon Hiltibidal
Director, Lifeway Adult Publishing

Jon Rodda
Art Director

Published by Lifeway Press® • © 2021 Greg Laurie

No part of this book may be reproduced or transmitted in any form or by any means, electronic or mechanical, including photocopying and recording, or by any information storage or retrieval system, except as may be expressly permitted in writing by the publisher. Requests for permission should be addressed in writing to Lifeway Press®; One Lifeway Plaza; Nashville, TN 37234.

ISBN 978-1-5359-9951-9 • Item 005823247

Dewey decimal classification: 269.24

Subject Headings:: REVIVALS / EVANGELISTIC WORK / SPIRITUAL LIFE

Unless otherwise indicated, all Scripture quotations are from the Christian Standard Bible®, Copyright © 2017 by Holman Bible Publishers. Used by permission. Christian Standard Bible® and CSB® are federally registered trademarks of Holman Bible Publishers.

Cover Design and Illustration: Josh Huffman

To order additional copies of this resource, write to Lifeway Resources Customer Service; One Lifeway Plaza; Nashville, TN 37234; fax 615-251-5933; call toll free 800-458-2772; order online at Lifeway.com; or email orderentry@lifeway.com.

Printed in the United States of America

Adult Ministry Publishing • Lifeway Resources • One Lifeway Plaza • Nashville, TN 37234

JESUS
REVOLUTION

ABOUT THE AUTHOR

Greg Laurie is the senior pastor of Harvest Christian Fellowship with campuses in California and Hawaii. He began his pastoral ministry at the age of 19 by leading a Bible study of 30 people. Since then, God has transformed that small group into a church of some 15,000 people, one of the largest in America.

In 1990, Laurie began holding large-scale public evangelistic events called Harvest Crusades. Since that time, more than 7.9 million people have participated in Harvest Crusades events in person or online. Laurie is the featured speaker of the nationally syndicated radio program A New Beginning. He also has a weekly television program on the Trinity Broadcasting Network and is the author of numerous books including *Johnny Cash: The Redemption of an American Icon*, *Steve McQueen: The Salvation of an American Icon*, *Live Love Fight*, *Tell Someone*, *The New Believer's Bible*, *Hope for Hurting Hearts*, and his autobiography, *Lost Boy*.

Greg has been married to Cathe Laurie for more than 40 years and they have two sons and five grandchildren.

THE
JESUS
REVOLUTION

God has always been interested in turning unlikely people into His fervent followers. Prostitutes and pagans, tax collectors, and tricksters. The more unlikely, the more it seems to please God and to demonstrate His power, might, and mercy. America in the 1960s and 1970s was full of unlikely people—men and women who had rejected the religion of their parents' generation, who didn't follow the rules, didn't fit in. The perfect setting for the greatest spiritual awakening of the 20th century. The Jesus Movement truly was an extraordinary time of mass revival, renewal, and reconciliation.

HOW TO GET THE MOST FROM THIS STUDY

This Bible study book includes six weeks of content for group and personal study.

GROUP SESSIONS

Regardless of what day of the week your group meets, each week of content begins with the group session. Each group session uses the following format to facilitate meaningful interaction among group members, with God's Word, and with the teaching of Pastor Greg.

START. This page includes questions to get the conversation started and to introduce the video teaching.

WATCH. This page includes key points from Pastor Greg's teaching, along with blanks for taking notes as participants watch the video.

DISCUSS. This page includes questions and statements that guide the group to respond to Pastor Greg's video teaching and to relevant Bible passages.

WRAP UP. This page leads you to apply the teaching and principles from Pastor Greg's teaching to your life.

THIS WEEK. This page prepares you for the week ahead.

PERSONAL STUDY

Each week provides five days of Bible study and learning activities for individual engagement between group sessions. These personal studies revisit stories, Scriptures, and themes introduced in the videos in order to understand and apply them on a personal level.

TIPS FOR LEADING A SMALL GROUP

Follow these guidelines to prepare for each group session.

PRAYERFULLY PREPARE

REVIEW. Review the weekly material and group questions ahead of time.

PRAY. Be intentional about praying for each person in the group.

Ask the Holy Spirit to work through you and the group discussion as you point to Jesus each week through God's Word.

MINIMIZE DISTRACTIONS

Create a comfortable environment. If group members are uncomfortable, they'll be distracted and therefore not engaged in the group experience. Plan ahead by considering these details:

SEATING   TEMPERATURE   LIGHTING

FOOD & DRINK   SURROUNDING NOISE

GENERAL CLEANLINESS

At best, thoughtfulness and hospitality show guests and group members they're welcome and valued in whatever environment you choose to gather. At worst, people may never notice your effort, but they're also not distracted. Do everything in your ability to help people focus on what's most important: connecting with God, with the Bible, and with one another.

INCLUDE OTHERS

Your goal is to foster a community in which people are welcome just as they are but encouraged to grow spiritually. Always be aware of opportunities to include any people who visit the group and to invite new people to join your group.

ENCOURAGE DISCUSSION

A good small-group experience has the following characteristics.

EVERYONE PARTICIPATES. Encourage everyone to ask questions, share responses, or read aloud.

NO ONE DOMINATES—NOT EVEN THE LEADER. Be sure that your time speaking as a leader takes up less than half of your time together as a group. Politely guide discussion if anyone dominates.

NOBODY IS RUSHED THROUGH QUESTIONS. Don't feel that a moment of silence is a bad thing. People often need time to think about their responses to questions they've just heard or to gain courage to share what God is stirring in their hearts.

INPUT IS AFFIRMED AND FOLLOWED UP. Make sure you point out something true or helpful in a response. Don't just move on. Build community with follow-up questions, asking how other people have experienced similar things or how a truth has shaped their understanding of God and the Scripture you're studying. People are less likely to speak up if they fear that you don't actually want to hear their answers or that you're looking for only a certain answer.

GOD AND HIS WORD ARE CENTRAL. Opinions and experiences can be helpful, but God has given us the truth. Trust God's Word to be the authority and God's Spirit to work in people's lives. You can't change anyone, but God can. Continually point people to the Word and to active steps of faith.

KEEP CONNECTING

Think of ways to connect with group members during the week.

Participation during the group session is always improved when members spend time connecting with one another outside the group sessions. The more people are comfortable with and involved in one another's lives, the more they'll look forward to being together. When people move beyond being friendly to truly being friends who form a community, they come to each session eager to engage instead of merely attending.

Encourage group members with thoughts, commitments, or questions from the session by connecting through these communication channels:

EMAILS   TEXTS   SOCIAL MEDIA

When possible, build deeper friendships by planning or spontaneously inviting group members to join you outside your regularly scheduled group time for activities like these:

MEALS   FUN ACTIVITIES

PROJECTS AROUND YOUR HOME,
CHURCH, OR COMMUNITY

Week 1

YOU SAY YOU WANT
A REVOLUTION?

START

Begin with a quick question to introduce the theme.
Answers can be funny or serious.

What is a recent challenge you've experienced?
What happened, and how did your life change as a result?

When have you done something that radically changed
your life? Why did you do it? What was the result?

Over the next six weeks, we'll see how God can move in our lives individually and in our culture at large. This first video will be a teaching on revival in general, what Greg experienced specifically during the Jesus Revolution, and how it could happen again today.

Pray that the Lord would give us eyes to see and ears to hear what He's saying to us in this moment.

WATCH

Use the space below to take notes as you watch the video for week 1.

DISCUSS

Pastor Greg ended by saying that if you want to see revival, start doing revival-like things. What does that mean?

What were some of the revival-like things mentioned in the video?

Of those revival-like things, which one comes most naturally? Which would take the most intentionality?

How is an awakening like a revival? Why is that a helpful distinction?

How does 2 Chronicles 7:14 help us understand revival?

How would you explain to someone who isn't in this group the significance of each distinctive from the Jesus Movement? Why is each one important to personal and church revival today?

1. Sense of Expectancy ("anointed listening")
2. The Bible was always taught.
3. People participated in worship.
4. People brought nonbelievers to church and invitations were extended.
5. Belief in the imminent return of Jesus
6. Work of the Holy Spirit

WRAP UP

Use these questions to wrap up your time together.

What does Deuteronomy 30:19 have to do with revival today?

What choice are you facing right now that could lead to personal revival and influence for Jesus?

Read Habakkuk 3:2.

What awesome things have you heard about the Lord doing in the Bible? In other people's lives?

What specifically would you want God to do in this generation?

Pray for God to "revive your work in these years," pouring out mercy in your lives individually, as a group, as a church, in order to bring awakening to the culture.

THIS WEEK

In 1968, the Beatles sang about how we all want to change the world. But in John Lennon's opinion, the people who said they wanted a revolution were going about it the wrong way—their actions and attitudes didn't line up with the values and goals of their own movement. For example, public protests were turning violent in the name of peace.

It's worth asking yourself the same question: Are you going about things the right way? Does your life match what you value? Awakening and revival sound great, but do you honestly want God to change the world? If so, are you ready to join His movement? He's done it before. He can do it again.

Don't worry, this won't be a guilt trip—it's a road map. You'll see where personal revolution begins and where it leads. In the following weeks, you'll begin to see what the Bible teaches about spiritual change and personal revolution. But here's the key—change is all about your relationship with Jesus.

This week, you'll read and reflect on what the Bible says about life. The next time you meet with your group, be prepared to share something that you learned or experienced during one of the following days:

DAY 1
Jesus and Treasure

DAY 2
Chasing the Wind

DAY 3
The Last Place Anyone Expects

DAY 4
Where is Your Hope?

DAY 5
Personal Reflection

Day 1
JESUS AND TREASURE

The kingdom of heaven is like treasure, buried in a field,
that a man found and reburied. Then in his joy he goes
and sells everything he has and buys that field.
MATTHEW 13:44

Can you imagine finding a buried treasure like the one Jesus described? Countless stories have been written about the adventures people experience in their pursuit of treasure. Jesus used this parable to describe the joy that comes from understanding He is King.

In the verse above, circle the word
describing the man's emotions.

Out of context, the man's behavior would seem irrational or foolish, but here it's obvious, joyful, and wise.

What does the man's emotion reveal about the treasure's value?

A few chapters later (see Matthew 19:16-22) Jesus meets a man who asks Him about the cost of being a disciple, except this man does not greet Jesus' invitation with joy.

At the end of this short conversation, what
invitation does Jesus offer the man?

What connection is Jesus making between eternal
life, treasure in heaven, and following Him?

Jesus wasn't saying that a person had to sell everything that they owned in order to gain eternal life. Throughout Scripture, people from across the income spectrum follow God—from helplessly poor (like widows) to immeasurably rich (like kings). Jesus challenged this particular man because He knew the man's possessions were keeping him from fully trusting God.

Did you notice the pride in the man's response to Jesus? The rich young man was laser-focused on—or distracted by—his own achievements. Jesus pointed the young ruler back to the Father. God desires more than your religious activity. He wants a relationship with you.

Religion is focused on earning an eternal reward through work. A relationship with God is about accepting eternal life as a gift—a treasure to be enjoyed. In Matthew 13, the man considered the kingdom of heaven as a greater treasure than anything he had. In Matthew 19, the man sulked away because he valued earthly things over heaven.

**What earthly pleasures keep you from following
Jesus completely and joyfully?**

The world doesn't need more self-righteous or "religious" people. It doesn't need anyone to make following Jesus seem more relevant or accessible. The world needs people who are full of a joy and freedom that can only be explained by the incomparable treasure found in Jesus. When people love Jesus with that kind of passion, their lives, families, jobs, schools, churches, and communities will be radically changed—now and for eternity.

> **Reflect on Jesus' revolutionary words in Matthew 6:19–34.
> Pray that you would trust in the goodness of God and seek
> His kingdom as your heart's greatest treasure.**

Day 2
CHASING THE WIND

I have seen all the things that are done under the sun and
have found everything to be futile, a pursuit of the wind.
ECCLESIASTES 1:14

The Old Testament book of Ecclesiastes has an unfortunate reputation of being "depressing." At first glance, it's easy to see why—just look at the verse above. Why would such a seemingly hopeless and negative commentary on life be included in the Bible?

Summarize Ecclesiastes 1:1–11 in a sentence or two.

The key to unlocking the wealth of knowledge hidden in the pages of Ecclesiastes is a simple phrase: under the sun. Those three words focus the reader's attention on the author's true message. Suddenly, the entire book can be seen clearly in light of the intentionally limited perspective—like a riddle that feels so obvious after learning the answer.

What does "under the sun" mean? How does this phrase
change your perspective on the Teacher's message?

Though the author is only identified as the Teacher, most people believe that King Solomon wrote Ecclesiastes. Solomon was the wisest, wealthiest, most powerful, and most successful man who ever lived. The rich young ruler Jesus met in yesterday's reading would pale in comparison to Solomon's greatness in every way. Unlike the rich young ruler, however, Solomon was not saddened by the thought of giving up his earthly things. Rather, he had accomplished, acquired, and experienced everything imaginable and found none of it to be satisfying or of true worth.

What are some of the things in this world that people treasure, value, or live for—believing that those things will give life meaning or significance?

Chances are that your list proves Solomon's point: there is nothing new under the sun. Since the beginning of time, no matter how advanced we think we're becoming, people keep repeating the same futile mistakes. We put "good" things on the throne of our hearts, living for treasures under the sun, rather than treasures in heaven and with God on the throne.

Check the boxes below for things you're prone to elevate from "good" to "God." Then read the related verses for the Teacher's sobering conclusions.

- ☐ **Wisdom and education (1:12–18)**
- ☐ **Pleasure and experience (2:1–3 and 8–11)**
- ☐ **Possessions and achievements (2:4–11)**
- ☐ **Work and skill (2:18–26)**
- ☐ **Power and justice (3:16–4:3)**
- ☐ **Wealth and legacy (4:4–6:7)**

When your hope and faith are in Jesus, the truth of Ecclesiastes is liberating not depressing. Like the man who eagerly sold everything to enjoy buried treasure, we know that the world is full of things that are good, but they're not God.

> **To end, read and reflect on the Teacher's final conclusion in Ecclesiastes 12:9–14. Pray that God would give you an eternal perspective rather than a heart set on everything under the sun.**

Day 3
THE LAST PLACE ANYONE EXPECTS

"Get up! Go to the great city of Nineveh and preach against it because their evil has come up before me."
JONAH 1:2

Chances are good that you're familiar with the story of Jonah. Most people could describe a Disney-like scene similar to Pinocchio in the belly of a whale. But rather than focusing on the reluctant prophet's time underwater, you'll journey through the whole story today. Don't worry, it's really good (and really short). As you read Jonah's story, consider how you can relate.

Read Jonah 1-2.

In chapter 1, Jonah tries to run from God's presence, fleeing to Tarshish, a city in the opposite direction of Ninevah.

When have you tried to run and hide from God or blatantly disobeyed Him?

In chapter 2, Jonah accepts the consequence of his sin and repents by turning back to the Lord.

What specific examples of God's all-powerful, all-knowing, always-present goodness stand out to you in chapters 1 and 2?

How have you experienced the undeserved grace of the all-powerful and all-knowing God?

In chapters 3–4, what did everyone do and why? Describe how God worked in the city of Ninevah. What was Jonah's response?

God's call on Jonah's life didn't change. His will for the people of Ninevah didn't change either. This was the most violent and sinful culture imaginable—the last place anyone expected a city-wide revival to happen. Even though God had just shown Jonah miraculous mercy, saving him with a big fish, he didn't want others to receive mercy for their rebellion. Like many of us, Jonah felt somehow entitled to God's grace while believing that other people didn't deserve any more chances.

Have you ever considered that God's will for your life isn't just about you? The grace, mercy, and goodness that He gives to you are not for you alone. The opportunity for salvation and blessing is even for "that person" who hurt you personally or "those people" who you may honestly want God to judge for their sinfulness in general.

Identify a needed change that only God can bring in each of the following.

Culture / "those" people:

Enemy / "that" person:

You:

If you've ever doubted God's ability or willingness to work through you, let Jonah encourage you. If you're discouraged that your family, friends, coworkers, or country seem to be hopelessly lost with no desire for God, take heart. If there's a person you've given up on, remember that if it can happen in Nineveh, it can happen anywhere!

To end, read and reflect on Jonah 2. Pray that God would give you a humble heart eager to be used for His purposes.

Day 4
WHERE IS YOUR HOPE?

Now faith is the reality of what is hoped for, the proof of what is not seen. For by it our ancestors won God's approval.
HEBREWS 11:1–2

Life changes quickly. Trends come and go. Teams win and lose. Relationships, careers, finances, policies, health, everything can change in an instant. You had to face this harsh reality when a pandemic swept through the world—not just in the news but affecting your own life. Over the past three days, your readings have led you through Scriptures that all point to the same crossroad. You have a question to answer that will determine the direction of your life now and forever: "Everybody puts their hope in something (or someone). Where is your hope? And where will it lead you in the end?"

Are you storing up treasures on earth or in heaven? Are you chasing the wind for fleeting moments under the sun or content knowing that everyone will face God in the end? Are you waiting for the gavel to drop in judgment of everything you think is wrong with the world or examining your own heart?

What does Hebrews 11:1–2 say about the right kind of hope?

The rest of Hebrews 11 is sometimes called "The Hall of Faith," offering a highlight reel of biblical history from the Old Testament. Take a few moments and read the rest of the chapter now. Not only does it provide a bigger perspective on life, but it is also truly inspiring.

Which example(s) from Hebrews 11 stood out to you personally?

How does this chapter (or the verses you identified) give you a "bigger" perspective on life?

The next chapter is directly linked to the incredible summary of men and women who put their hope in God and experienced incredible movements of His power as a result. A good rule of thumb for reading and studying the Bible is to ask yourself, "What is 'therefore' there for?"

Read Hebrews 12:1–2. How should you respond to the lives of real men and women recorded in your Bible?

How do these men and women ultimately point us to Jesus Christ?

It's tempting to dismiss miracles as something God did back in biblical times. But the Bible isn't a book of fairytales, myths, and legends. The pages of Scripture include the experiences of real men, women, and children. And when you put your hope in Christ, this is your family history too. The people in Hebrews 11 are your ancestors through your common faith.

Write Hebrews 13:8 in the space below.

Based on that reality, write a personal declaration of hope starting with "therefore."

Read and reflect on the rally cry of Joshua found in Joshua 24:15 (his life was alluded to in Hebrews 11:30). Pray for faith that pleases the Lord—a confident hope in His power and goodness.

Day 5
PERSONAL REFLECTION

Everybody processes thoughts and feelings differently—it's part of how God created us uniquely. Day 5 of each week is designed to give you room to be yourself.

For example: maybe you're not even sure what you think or how you feel until you start writing. You might like to doodle or could even be a talented artist who best expresses yourself visually. Perhaps you resonate deeply with music or poetry. Whatever works for you—journaling, drawing, writing poetry, favorite song lyrics, or a prayer—invite the Spirit to make this a personal time of reflection.

Use this space to reflect on everything you've been reading this week about life.

What specific truths or general ideas
have been meaningful to you?

Week 2

WHO IS THE SPIRIT?

START

Begin with a quick review and time of sharing. Be mindful of how God is at work in your life.

What is something that you learned or experienced in a new way during one of the daily readings last week?

What was your biggest takeaway from Greg's teaching last week?

Only God can bring spiritual awakening and revival. The Holy Spirit convicts, convinces, and empowers people for a radically new life with Jesus.

Pray for the Spirit to move in your hearts as "anointed listeners" to the Word of God today.

WATCH

Use the space below to take notes as you watch the video for week 2.

DISCUSS

Greg ended by saying that we don't need another Pentecost any more than we need another Calvary—the same power is available for believers today. What does that mean?

Read Romans 8:11. How does it change your perspective as a follower of Jesus, knowing that you have the same Spirit that raised Christ and empowered His disciples at Pentecost?

Why is it important to recognize the ordinary and diverse backgrounds of Jesus' disciples?

Read Acts 1:8. How did Greg explain the word "power" in this verse?

What did the Spirit's power enable the disciples to do? Why is that important to keep in mind as Christians?

The Book of Acts has three vital ingredients working together: The Spirit of God ... working through the Word of God ... in the hearts of God's people. Why do you think the Spirit is often left out of the equation today?

It's easy to feel like revival and powerful movements of the Spirit won't happen again. What did Greg say about emotions and obedience based on Ephesians 5:18?

WRAP UP

Remember the three ways that the Spirit works in our lives today:

1. The Holy Spirit convicts us of sin and convinces us of truth.

2. The Holy Spirit empowers us to be witnesses of the gospel.

3. The Holy Spirit enables a personal relationship with Jesus.

What was personally convicting or convincing in today's teaching?

Who do you know that is not yet a believer in Jesus?

What steps can you take to "be filled with the Holy Spirit" this week?

THIS WEEK

The Spirit is not some spooky thing reserved for fanatical behavior, nor is it merely a doctrinal box to check off the list of Christian beliefs. In fact, the Spirit is not a "thing" or an "it" at all. The Spirit is a Person, a "He." And He's fully God, every bit as much as Jesus is God.

The Spirit is God's presence and power within you—the very same power that raised Christ from the dead. What could be more amazing and encouraging than that? After all of the soul-searching that you did last week, counting the cost of a lifelong adventure with Jesus, you'll start getting to know your travel companion now. The Holy Spirit has been with you since the beginning and will be with you every step of the way, guiding and empowering you for the revolutionary life of a Christ-follower.

This week, you'll read and reflect on what the Bible says about the Spirit. Be prepared to share something with your group from one of the following days:

DAY 1
Jesus and the Spirit

DAY 2
Continually Filled

DAY 3
You are the Temple

DAY 4
The Greatest Gift

DAY 5
Personal Reflection

Day 1
JESUS AND THE SPIRIT

*I am telling you the truth. It is for your benefit that
I go away, because if I don't go away the Counselor
will not come to you. If I go, I will send him to you.*
JOHN 16:7

Do you really believe what Jesus said—that it's even better for you to have the Holy Spirit than for Jesus to be physically present, walking and talking on the earth today? That's a pretty huge reality to wrap your heart and mind around.

If you're ever going to experience awakening and revival in your church, community, or nation, then it must start with the Holy Spirit. The same is true for your own life. In fact, all Christian activity begins with the Holy Spirit. Therefore, it's pretty important to know the third person of the Trinity.

In the verse above, Jesus taught to His disciples on the night before His crucifixion. John chapters 14–17 are often referred to as the Farewell Discourse. One of the primary emphases of Jesus' final teaching—the last thing He wanted to be sure they understood before He would be killed and they'd be wondering what to do about this revolution that seemed to be growing—was introducing them to the Holy Spirit.

**Who is the Spirit according to the following verses?
What key phrases, roles, or activities mentioned
by Jesus help you better know the Spirit?**

John 14:15-18

John 14:23-26

John 15:26–27

John 16:7–11

John 16:13–14

The original Greek word used for the Spirit in these passages is so rich in meaning and nuance that your English translation of the Bible may use any number of reasonable options: "Comforter" (KJV), "Counselor" (NIV, CSB), "Advocate" (NRSV, New Living Translation), or "Helper" (ESV, NASB). All of those names relay the original idea of someone who comes alongside someone else. More specifically, the term was often used in a legal or judicial setting, so the Holy Spirit is someone who was sent to be your personal helper and representative, declaring your freedom from guilt and condemnation, and aiding in your knowledge of truth and acts of righteousness.

**How do these passages help you understand
your relationship with the Spirit?**

**Why might Jesus have wanted His disciples to know
those things about the Spirit before He was crucified?**

**Read and reflect on Jesus's final words after His resurrection in
Acts 1:1–11. Pray for an awareness of the Spirit's presence and power.**

Day 2
CONTINUALLY FILLED

*So don't be foolish, but understand what the Lord's
will is. And don't get drunk with wine, which leads
to reckless living, but be filled by the Spirit.*
EPHESIANS 5:17–18

Before ascending into heaven (the verses you read and reflected on for the closing prayer yesterday), Jesus promised His disciples that they would "receive power when the Holy Spirit has come on you" (Acts 1:8), empowering them to be His witnesses. Imagine what the disciples must have been wondering as they waited for the Holy Spirit. What would happen? How would they know it was time to stop waiting and to start witnessing?

They experienced what Jesus promised on Pentecost, the Jewish festival celebrating the beginning of a new wheat harvest, 50 days after Passover. The Bible says that the sound of a mighty wind came from heaven, tongues of fire spread out over the disciples' heads, and "they were all filled with the Holy Spirit" (Acts 2:4). Then they started talking and people from every nation that had gathered for the festival were amazed and confused: "we hear them declaring the magnificent acts of God in our own tongues" (Acts 2:11). The best answer that people could offer for the strange event was that the disciples were drunk (Acts 2:12).

> **It's amazing what we'd rather believe than facing the
> reality of the Spirit's work in our lives. What excuses
> have you heard or given to explain spiritual activity?**

People suddenly speaking and hearing in multiple foreign languages wasn't the only miraculous event. The apostle Peter was literally about to have a personal transformation. Immediately before the Farewell Discourse, Jesus predicted that Peter would deny Him three times that same night—which he did after Jesus' arrest. After being filled with the Spirit at Pentecost, Peter boldly stood and publicly delivered the first sermon and invitation for sinners to respond to the gospel of Jesus in faith for their salvation!

**According to Peter in Acts 2:36–39, how does
a person receive the Holy Spirit?**

We don't need another Pentecost any more than we need another crucifixion, resurrection, or ascension. Anyone of any ethnicity in any generation who responds to the gospel with repentance and faith for salvation receives the Holy Spirit. So if believers in Jesus already have the Spirit upon conversion, what does it mean to "be filled by the Spirit" in today's opening verse?

Two things are important to understand this biblical command. And yes, it is a command (see verse 18)! First, to "get drunk" is to give control of yourself over to the influence and power of alcohol's effects on your body and mind. Therefore, God's Word says that you should give yourself over to the influence and power of the Spirit so that your thoughts, desires, and behavior will be affected for holiness.

Second, the Greek word used in Ephesians 5:18 communicates a continual, ongoing process of being filled. Believers receive the Spirit of God at the moment of salvation but must choose to walk with the Spirit daily—choosing His desires over the desires of your flesh (Romans 8:5-8). Walking with the Spirit is the daily pursuit of the Christian.

**On a scale of 1–10 (1 = not at all, 10 = completely)
how open are you to the Spirit? How willing are you
to let Him have complete control of your life?**

1   2   3   4   5   6   7   8   9   10

**What else fills and influences your thoughts,
feelings, behaviors, and activities?**

**Read and reflect on Galatians 5:16–26. Confess any sin and pray
that your life would be overflowing and fruitful in the Spirit.**

Day 3
YOU ARE THE TEMPLE

*Don't you know that your body is a temple of the Holy Spirit
who is in you, whom you have from God? You are not your own,
for you were bought at a price. So glorify God with your body.*
1 CORINTHIANS 6:19–20

As a Christian, you have a personal relationship with the Holy Spirit. Have you ever thought about it that way? You've most likely heard or talked about a relationship with God the Father or a relationship with Jesus, the Son, but the Holy Spirit usually gets treated as either a theological box to check—yes, I believe in the Holy Spirit as the third and equal person of God in the Trinity—or as a power to tap into like a Christian Jedi Force, showing up in all kinds of unusual ways. The Bible, on the other hand, describes someone so much more personal than those two extremes.

Romans 8 is one of the greatest chapters in the Bible about your relationship with the Spirit:

**Read Romans 8:1-39 and write down key
truths from the following verses:.**

**What do you have (and not have) in the
Spirit of life in Christ (1–2)?**

How does the Spirit change your life (6–11)?

How does the Spirit change your identity (14–17)?

How does the Spirit change your perspective (18–25)?

How does the Spirit help our growth in maturity(26–30)?

What is the result of your relationship (31–39)?

In Day 1 and 2, you saw that the Holy Spirit is a multi-faceted helper sent to be with you, that you receive the Spirit along with your salvation, and that you can be more and less under the influence of His power and presence. Today you see the responsibility that comes with this incredible privilege.

"No condemnation in Christ" and His "law of freedom" doesn't mean that you can do whatever you want. The Holy Spirit isn't your "get out of jail free" card.

According to 1 Corinthians 6:12–15 and 19–20, why do the choices that you make with your body have spiritual significance?

Since your body is the temple, you don't have to go somewhere to meet with God. How can you honor His Spirit living in you?

Since the same Spirit that raised Christ from the dead lives inside you, no habit or addiction is impossible to overcome.

What negative things can you stop doing by the power of the Spirit?

Read and reflect on Romans 8, focusing on any verses that spoke to you personally as you read them earlier. Pray that the Spirit would intercede on your behalf, growing you in holiness as a living temple.

Day 4
THE GREATEST GIFT

Now there are different gifts, but the same Spirit. There are different ministries, but the same Lord. And there are different activities, but the same God produces each gift in each person.
1 CORINTHIANS 12:4-6

The Spirit—your Counselor, Advocate, Helper, and Friend—brings housewarming gifts as He dwells within you. In addition to getting to know who He is, what He does, where He lives, and when He moves in, it's important to recognize what He gives.

Identifying spiritual gifts is more than a Christian version of a personality assessment. In the opening verse above, the Apostle Paul says there is only one spiritual "type" of Christian. You share a common bond with every Christian on the planet through the Spirit within you.

What is the first thing that the Spirit gives you according to 1 Corinthians 12:1-3?

Those verses also reveal that people have been interested in (and confused by) spiritual gifts since the beginning of church history. God created you in a particular way and knows you inside and out, including your temperament, tendencies, and talents. He also gifted you in ways above and beyond your natural abilities. The first supernatural gift you've been given is the power to confess in faith, "Jesus is Lord."

Write 1 Corinthians 12:7 in the space below.

Spiritual gifts point you to Christ, and then they point you to others. They're not about becoming a "better you." They're for becoming a better "us."

Paul uses a vivid word picture (with a sense of humor) to make his point about spiritual gifts being for the "common good" of the Christian community.

What imagery is used in 1 Corinthians 12:12-31 and what are the main points?

What is the greatest gift according to 1 Corinthians 13?

You may be surprised to realize that those verses are talking about spiritual gifts since they are so often read at weddings.

In the space below, "Love is..." lists the characteristics of mature Christian love.

LOVE is...

Read and reflect on Jesus' words in John 13:34-35. Pray that the Spirit will mature you and fill you with Christlike love for others.

Day 5
PERSONAL REFLECTION

Use this space to reflect on everything you've been reading this week about the Spirit.

**What specific truths or general ideas
have been meaningful to you?**

Week 3

HOW DO WE PRAY?

START

Begin with a quick review and time of sharing. Be mindful of how God is at work in your life.

What is something that you learned or experienced in a new way during last week's reading?

What was your biggest takeaway from last week's video teaching or discussion?

Revival always starts with putting ourselves in a posture of dependence upon God. The Spirit-filled life is fueled through continual prayer, turning from ourselves and toward the Lord.

Pray that God would give each of you a humble heart of passionate prayer.

WATCH

Use the space below to take notes as you watch the video for week 3

DISCUSS

Greg ended with R.A. Torrey's "prescription" for revival: People getting right with God, binding themselves together in prayer, and making themselves available to be used by God. How do these three things add up to revival in any context? How is prayer vital to all three things?

Historically, revivals in America have followed major hardships or crisis—Revolutionary War, Wild West, Stock Market Crash, Vietnam and assassinations of the 1960s. How might these cultural events revive churches and awaken culture?

During America's second great awakening, Charles Finney, said: "revival is nothing more or less than the new beginning of obedience to God." What has God used in your own life to show you your need for Him, for prayer, and for obedience?

Read Nehemiah 9:1-2. Why is confession such an important part of prayer?

Notice that God's people didn't point out the sins of pagan cultures around them but confessed their own sins. How does that relate to Greg's comment in the video: "revival happens when God gets so sick and tired of being misrepresented that He shows up himself." What is an example of confessing our own sin as God's people today?

What are sins of commission and omission? Give examples of both.

WRAP UP

Use these questions to wrap up your time together.

Revival starts with us. We have to get back to the basics.
What did Greg say about the 3 R's of Revival?

1. Remember
2. Repent
3. Repeat

What did the evangelist Billy Sunday say about taking a bath?
How does it relate to prayer?

Read Matthew 6:9-14. Share an important insight on
the "basics" of prayer from each verse.

What practices have you found helpful in prayer?

What gets in the way of prayer?

How can we pray for one another right now?

THIS WEEK

All movements of God start with prayer.

This is the first practical and powerful step of Spirit-filled living and revival. Logically, how can we be aware of what God is doing and join Him in it if we're not spending time with Him? Relationships require communication—talking and listening to one another. That's all prayer is—talking to God, getting to know Him, and listening to what He tells us.

Have you ever thought about what an incredible blessing it is to speak with God? Not only can you talk to Him, but He also wants you to know Him on a deeply personal level. The God of the universe invites you into a relationship with Him. Prayer isn't some mysterious and difficult ritual to master; it's a privilege worth making a regular part of your daily routine and rhythm in life.

This week, you'll read and reflect on what the Bible says about prayer. Be prepared to share something with your group from one of the following days:

DAY 1
Jesus and Our Father

DAY 2
On Earth as it is in Heaven

DAY 3
Give Us Today Our Daily Bread

DAY 4
Forgive Us and Deliver Us

DAY 5
Personal Reflection

Day 1
JESUS AND OUR FATHER

Therefore, you should pray like this:
Our Father in heaven,
your name be honored as holy.
MATTHEW 6:9

Of all the things that Jesus could have taught His disciples about prayer, the first thing that He chose to emphasize was our personal relationship with God. He's not a genie in a bottle to be manipulated with magic words, a spiritual force to tap into with practice, or an unapproachable deity to appease. He's our Father.

Which one of these two realities do you lean toward in your view of God?

Father   holy

How does it affect the way you treat prayer if you see God as:

Father (only):

_____

Holy (only):

_____

Both:

_____

Circle the words that you associate with prayer.

awkward	awesome	blessing	burden
confession	conversation	duty	delight
emergency	essential	mysterious	personal
powerful	pointless	relationship	requests
	responsibility	ritual	

It was a common practice in Jesus' day for disciples to not only learn the teachings of a rabbi but also to pray like a rabbi. How a disciple understands the Scriptures will always impact the way they interact with God personally.

Are you more prone to spend time in Scripture, in prayer, both, or neither? What do your tendencies suggest about your relationship with God?

Now consider how you interact, not just how often. What does the way that you interact with Scripture reveal about your view of God?

What do your prayers reveal about your view of God?

You may or may not have had a good earthly example of a Father. No matter what your earthly Father is like, your heavenly Father is perfect in all of His ways. Scripture uses the word "Abba" to describe your relationship with God. In biblical times, "Abba" was a term that some people translate as "Dad" or "Daddy," revealing trust, love, and respect in the most personal way.

You have a Father in heaven. He is perfectly holy. He loves you personally. As you grow in this relationship, your life will never be the same. Prayer, then, becomes all about getting to know God, not getting something from Him.

To end, read and reflect on Romans 8:14–16. Pray that Holy Spirit would help you embrace your identity as a child of God and the relationship with God as your holy Abba, Father.

Day 2
ON EARTH AS IT IS IN HEAVEN

Your kingdom come.
Your will be done
on earth as it is in heaven.
MATTHEW 6:10

The second phrase of Jesus' model prayer for His disciples summed up His earthly ministry. What better description is there of the Christian life? God's kingdom is God's rule in this world and the world to come. Jesus' life inaugurated the kingdom of God on earth. Jesus' miracles, teachings, and personal example were previews of God's will being done on earth.

How did Matthew summarize the message Jesus "began to preach"? Rewrite Jesus' words from Matthew 4:17 into the space below.

What does repentance have to do with the kingdom and will of God?

Now, look at Jesus' personal example near the end of His ministry, praying before His arrest and crucifixion.

What did Jesus repeatedly pray in Matthew 26:36–46?

Notice that Jesus expressed His natural human desire to our heavenly Father. Just because He wanted to do what honored God didn't mean it was easy. Jesus knew He was heading to the cross to take on the sins of the world—including ours. Beyond the physical and emotional suffering that He was about to endure through betrayal, injustice, humiliation, torture, and death, Jesus was about to experience the reality of God's righteous judgment on sin. But He trusted, obeyed, and desired God's will above His own.

What is most consuming your thoughts and prayers lately?

Write a simple prayer, expressing your desire but also expressing your trust in God's will, whatever that means.

What does it look like for God's kingdom to come and His will to be done? Most simply, it means that you desire for God's holiness to be honored in this world and for Him to be loved, trusted, and obeyed by all people as their Father. This starts in your own life.

You have to believe that God and His will are truly more desirable than your own plans, wants, comforts, etc. A Jesus Revolution takes place when you want whatever God wants because He is that good. When you believe that God's will is not only "right" but is truly "best," your heart begins to look more like Jesus'.

Many people are skeptical of Christians. Yet many of those same people would say that they respect and admire Jesus. For these folks to see Jesus we need Christians with a revolutionary understanding of the Christian life. We need Christians committed to God's agenda and His kingdom rather than their own. This is what Jesus lived, died, rose again, and is coming back for: God's kingdom, not ours. This is what a watching world needs to see in our day-to-day lives.

> **To end, read and reflect on Matthew 26:36–46.**
> **Ask God to help you stay alert in prayer and to desire**
> **God's kingdom and will above your own.**

Day 3
GIVE US TODAY OUR DAILY BREAD

Give us today our daily bread.
MATTHEW 6:11

This is where a lot of people's prayers tend to start and end: asking for things. We've all asked God to give us something we'd like or to help us out of a situation that we don't like. Often, these sorts of prayers include promises that are rarely kept as we try to bargain with God: "If you do this for me, then I promise I'll never do this again... or I'll start doing that instead." Or whatever our personal tendency is in negotiation tactics.

You don't have to negotiate with God, and that's good news. Honestly, you don't have any ability to bargain with Him. Trying to do this is natural but ultimately indicates a lack of faith.

What are some examples of prayers that were really just you trying to make a deal with God to get what you want?

What promises have you made in desperate moments of trying to get God to help you? Did you keep your promises?

You can be encouraged to see that Jesus taught His disciples to bring their requests to God. It's not selfish to ask for what we need or even what we want. As our heavenly Father, He is both willing and able to take perfect care of His children. He doesn't need our promises or bargains to be faithful.

How would you summarize Jesus' teaching in Matthew 7:9–11?

During the time of Moses, God led the children of Israel out of captivity from Egypt. They had to learn to trust the goodness of God and His will for them. He not only saved them, He literally provided for them. One of the ways that the Lord met their needs while also reminding everyone of His goodness was to miraculously provide bread from heaven each morning (except for on the Sabbath when He would provide a double portion on the morning before). They called this heavenly bread "manna," which means, "what is it?" No earthly explanation could be given for what they experienced.

During Jesus' ministry, people tried to manipulate Him by challenging Him to provide them with bread like Moses had done (John 6). On at least two occasions, we know that Jesus did miraculously multiply bread to feed huge crowds that had gathered to hear His teaching and to see what miracles He would do. But Jesus wouldn't be manipulated or bargained with. Instead, He invited people into a relationship with God through faith in Him. He wanted to meet both their temporary physical needs and their eternal spiritual needs—both matter to our heavenly Father and to His Son.

**What did James, the half-brother of Jesus, say
about God's provision in James 1:17?**

**In James 5:13–18, what did he say about the
power of prayer and specific requests?**

> **To end, read and reflect on Matthew 6:25–34. Ask God to meet all
> of your needs and trust that He will do so out of His love for you.**

Day 4
FORGIVE US AND DELIVER US

And forgive us our debts,
as we also have forgiven our debtors.
And do not bring us into temptation,
but deliver us from the evil one.
MATTHEW 6:12–13

Christianity is not just about "getting saved." Following Jesus is a daily journey and a life of faith. But there is a moment when you are "born again" into the family of God, while you also continue to grow in maturity and Christlikeness. Once God is your heavenly Father through faith in His Son, Jesus, you will always be His child. Once you put your faith in Jesus, you are "forgiven" in Christ—forever. Nothing can change that. You have entered into the kingdom of God as part of His family (John 3:3–8).

What does John 3:16–21 teach about
forgiveness and condemnation?

Do you know your spiritual birthday? When did you first
confess your sin to God, asking for His forgiveness?

As you learn to trust your heavenly Father in every area of your life, you will also begin to recognize that, like the children of Israel who ate manna in the wilderness, you're not always grateful for your new freedom. You're tempted to "go back" to the bondage of sin. But temptation is a liar. It never delivers on its promise.

Read Numbers 11:4–6. What blessings do you take for granted in your own life?

The Israelites remembered "free fish" and a variety of foods in Egypt, but in reality, they were slaves having barely enough to survive their forced labor. This is the deadly poison of temptation and sin. We believe things that aren't true, thinking that we'd be better off or that giving in to this desire would be worth it in our particular circumstance.

Identify some lies (excuses) that try to justify sin in today's world.

The Bible is clear; God never leads you into temptation. Temptation comes from your own desires (James 1:13–15). We never have a valid excuse.

Write 1 Corinthians 10:13 in the space below.

A Christian is never obligated to sin; God will always provide a way out of temptation so that by the Spirit's power, you may choose God's will over sin.

What temptations are strongest in your life?

What are some "ways out" when you are under temptation?

To end, read and reflect on James 1:13–17. Pray for the Spirit to give you humility and a desire to reflect your heavenly Father's holiness. Ask God's forgiveness for specific sins in your own life.

JESUS
REVOLUTION

Day 5
PERSONAL REFLECTION

Use this space to reflect on everything you've been reading this week about prayer.

What specific truths or general ideas
have been meaningful to you?

Week 4

WHAT IS THE BIBLE?

START

Begin with a quick review and time of sharing. Be mindful of how God is at work in your life.

What is something that you learned or experienced in a new way during last week's reading?

What was your biggest takeaway from last week's video teaching or discussion?

Prayer and the Bible go hand-in-hand for the Spirit-filled follower of Jesus. In order to be in a living relationship with Jesus means letting God's Word tell us who He really is.

Pray that the Spirit would give you a hunger for the life-changing truth of God's Word.

WATCH

Use the space below to take notes as you watch the video for week 4.

DISCUSS

Why is it important to consider whether or not we have a true relationship with Jesus?

How is a right understanding of the Bible related to personal faith in Jesus?

How was the Bible viewed during the Jesus Revolution, according to Time Magazine? How is this attitude different from the one represented by Jefferson's Bible?

What are some common views of the Bible in our culture? What do you believe about the Bible?

Read Psalm 19:7-11. How would you summarize the psalmist's attitude toward Scripture?

What was your biggest takeaway from each of the following characteristics of the Bible?

1. Word of God is perfect
2. Word of God revives us
3. Word of God gives wisdom
4. Word of God is right
5. Word of God makes you happy
6. Word of God reveals Jesus
7. Word of God points to eternal life

WRAP UP

Use the following to wrap up your time together.

How should the truth of 2 Timothy 3:16-17 affect our attitude toward God's Word?

What has helped you develop a good habit of enjoying time in God's Word?

When do you most often read the Bible? Why is that a good time for you?

What verses have you memorized? Why did you choose them?
How have they helped you?

THIS WEEK

Last week you began to unpack the incredible gift of prayer you've been given through your relationship with God. It's a two-way conversation with your heavenly Father where you speak and listen to Him. Even though it's obviously different than other personal conversations, you know how conversation works in general and Jesus taught His disciples—including you—how to talk to God specifically. The listening part of prayer takes a little more practice. Fortunately, you have God's Word in writing. The main way you listen to God, even in prayer, is by knowing what He said in Scripture.

The Bible is not a book that was written so that people could know about God and grow in their practice of religion for Him. The Bible contains the words that God has given so that people could know Him and grow in their relationships with Him.

Knowing what the Bible says is the first step toward a closer relationship with God—Father, Son, and Holy Spirit. The Christian life is one of following Jesus in obedience, love, joy, satisfaction, and experiencing His power.

This week, you'll read and reflect on what the Bible says about Scripture. Be prepared to share something with your group from one of the following days:

DAY 1
Jesus and Wisdom

DAY 2
Strength Under Temptation

DAY 3
His Thoughts > Our Thoughts

DAY 4
The Power of the Gospel

DAY 5
Personal Reflection

Day 1
JESUS AND WISDOM

Therefore, everyone who hears these words of mine and acts on them will be like a wise man who built his house on the rock.
MATTHEW 7:24

Jesus once told a story comparing and contrasting a wise man and a foolish man. If you grew up in church or have children of your own, you probably know a song and maybe hand motions for what happens to both men when "the rains came down and floods came up."

First, Jesus (and therefore the children's song) start with the wise man.

What sobering question did Jesus ask in Luke 6:46?

What three steps of wisdom does Jesus describe in Luke 6:47?

1.

2.

3.

How does Jesus connect hearing and obeying His commands?

How does knowing and obeying the teachings of Jesus help you survive even the roughest of storms in life?

If you were a kid singing about the wise man, you'd be flexing your muscles right now to indicate the strength found in obedience to Christ. True faith in Jesus involves coming to Him, hearing from Him, and obeying Him. The first two steps are easy. It's the last step that trips us up. Are you willing to trust and obey Jesus in your life, right now? Will you "build" your life on the firm foundation of true faith—hearing God's Word and doing what it says?

**In Luke 6:49, another man built his house on the sand.
According to Jesus, what made the man foolish?**

With a loud clap of the hands, kids proclaim: "SPLAT!" or "CRASH!" as the inevitable fate of the foolish man's house that was built upon the sand. While the song is cute and a lot of fun for kids, it contains a powerful promise and a serious warning for us as adults.

Notice that it wasn't a lack of knowledge that made the man foolish. He wasn't ignorant. He was disobedient, apathetic, and unimpressed with Jesus' teaching. The foolish man knew the truth but didn't put his faith in Jesus. Christ says that it's not enough to know the truth about Jesus or to believe that the Bible is the Word of God.

Dig deep in your heart and ask yourself the hard questions:

Where am I not obeying Jesus?

Where am I not doing what the Bible says?

> **To end, read and reflect on Proverbs 3:5-6. Pray for the Spirit to help you discern the foundational beliefs that you're building your life upon. Ask for His help to trust and obey.**

Day 2
STRENGTH UNDER TEMPTATION

*[Jesus] answered, "It is written: Man must not live on bread
alone but on every word that comes from the mouth of God."*
MATTHEW 4:4

Some people like to say that God will never give you more than you can handle. That simply isn't true. The Bible is full of stories about people facing tasks that were completely beyond their ability to handle—on their own.

What the Bible does promise is that God will always be with you through the power and presence of the Spirit (Week 2) and that He will not allow you to be trapped in temptation without a way out (Week 3). You will always have an escape. You always have the strength you need to do the right thing, if you ask for it.

**How do you handle temptation? What are some
of your escape plans or strategies?**

**Think about the last time you were tempted.
Did you give in to temptation? (Circle answer.)**

Yes   No

What went through your head as you faced that temptation?

The Gospels are clear that Jesus was truly God and truly man. While this is a mystery that we can't fully wrap our minds around, we can know for certain and rest assured that Jesus' human experience included temptation.

Not only did He face temptations throughout His daily life as a child, teen-ager, and young adult, Jesus faced an intense season of temptation as He began His earthly ministry around the age of 30.

What does the fact that Jesus was tempted teach you?

**What can you learn from the fact that His most
explicit season of temptation followed His
baptism and came before His ministry?**

In Matthew 4:1–11, how did Jesus respond to temptation?

**What is a favorite verse that you've memorized?
How can it help you In the face of temptation?**

Knowing the Word of God is vital. Familiarizing yourself with the whole Bible helps you to know when it is being taken out of context and twisted to justify sin. Jesus showed you how to take a strong stand against temptation. He had Scripture memorized. When facing temptation, the truth of God's Word immediately provided Jesus with the strength and wisdom to resist the devil's temptation. Not only does the Lord give you daily bread, He gives you the bread of life through His Word.

**To end, read and reflect on Ephesians 6:10–17.
Ask God to help you stand strong against temptation and
to learn how to rightly handle the sword of the Spirit—
God's Word—your weapon in spiritual warfare.**

Day 3
HIS THOUGHTS >
OUR THOUGHTS

*For as heaven is higher than earth, so my ways are higher
than your ways, and my thoughts than your thoughts.*
ISAIAH 55:9

**What fills your mind on a regular basis? Check all that
apply and write specific examples to the side**

☐ Social media: _____   ☐ Bible study/prayer: _____

☐ Video clips: _____   ☐ Sermons _____

☐ Podcasts/radio: _____   ☐ Corporate worship: _____

☐ Books/Audiobooks: _____   ☐ Classes/seminars: _____

☐ News media: _____   ☐ Conversations: _____

☐ Movies/shows/sports: _____   ☐ Text/email: _____

☐ Music: _____   ☐ Other: _____

**Using your answers above, create a pie chart estimating the amount
of time spent each day filling your mind with various thoughts.**

The point of the previous exercises is not to judge the amount of time spent with any particular form of media or communication. (However, allow the Spirit to convict or encourage you personally in any area that He may be at work in you). The intent is to simply bring awareness that we are constantly filling our minds with information.

Like Jesus during His temptation, the prophet Isaiah used the imagery of eating and drinking in relation to the life-giving and all-sufficient words of God. A few chapters after one of the most descriptive prophesies of Christ as the "suffering servant," something that nobody expected (Isa. 52), God reminded His people of the nature and power of His words.

What does Isaiah 55:1–7 reveal about life in our own wisdom?

What does it reveal about God's desire for us?

What does Isaiah 55:8–11 reveal about the wisdom of God?

When you spend time reading, memorizing, and reflecting on Scripture, you are filling your mind with the thoughts of God. It's vital that you renew your minds daily and corporately—as a Christian and as a part of the church, the body of Christ. If your opinion doesn't match the Bible—change your mind. Don't try to use Scripture to support your own opinions. Let the power of God's Word accomplish His will in and through you. He has given us the Bible to know and experience new life in Christ.

To end, read and reflect on Romans 12:1–2. Ask the Holy Spirit to renew your mind through the Word of God so that your thoughts reflect God's will instead of the culture's current preferences.

Day 4
THE POWER OF THE GOSPEL

For I am not ashamed of the gospel, because it is the power of God for salvation to everyone who believes, first to the Jew, and also to the Greek.
ROMANS 1:16

Now that's a verse worthy of defining your identity and shaping your outlook on life. Not only does it speak to personal conviction in boldly identifying with the life-changing power of the gospel, it also clarifies purpose and mission: to reach all people with the message of salvation in Jesus Christ. Whether in the suburbs or inner city, rich or poor, black or white, speaking English or Spanish, Republican or Democrat, or any other label that we may apply to people, the gospel is for everyone and can change anyone.

Are there any specific individuals or general groups of people that you treat as unsavable (they'll never change)?

Even if you wouldn't use the word "ashamed," when are you most uncomfortable with being identified as a Christian or speaking about your faith?

If ever there was a time in American history that resembled the 1960's and 1970's, it's right now. People everywhere are eager for change. They want things to be right. They don't know who or what to believe. The answer to our pain and problems as a culture are not political or social revolutions. Certainly, there are practical changes that shape a society for better or worse, but for a culture to change people have to change, and for people to change, hearts have to change. Only the gospel of Jesus, preserved faithfully in the Bible, can change people's hearts.

It's not all "bad" news today. A lot of people are doing wonderful things with good intentions and some even have good results. But surely we've learned in recent days how quickly things can change.

What does Isaiah 40:6–8 say about the goodness of humanity?

On a scale of 1–10 (1 = not at all, 10 = completely) how confident are you in the power of God to transform your life and the lives of people around you?

1   2   3   4   5   6   7   8   9   10

You may not have the same platform as a pastor or an evangelist, but you have the same power of the same gospel that faithful men and women have had for 2000 years. You have the same Scripture that faithful men and women have had for even longer. Revival and revolution are just as possible today as they were at any point in human history.

Based on what you've read this week about the power of God's Word, what are you doing in each of the following practices:

☐ Reading the Bible
☐ Memorizing Bible verses
☐ Praying biblical promises
☐ Thinking about Scripture
☐ Singing biblical truth
☐ Talking about the gospel
☐ Applying biblical commands

To end, read and reflect on 2 Timothy 3:16–17. Pray for God's help in understanding and applying His Word to your life.

Day 5
PERSONAL REFLECTION

Use this space to reflect on everything you've been reading this week about the Bible.

**What specific truths or general ideas
have been meaningful to you?**

_____

_____

_____

_____

_____

_____

_____

_____

_____

_____

_____

_____

_____

_____

_____

Week 5

WHO GOES TO HEAVEN?

START

Begin with a quick review and time of sharing. Be mindful of how God is at work in your life.

What is something that you learned or experienced in a new way during last week's reading?

What was your biggest takeaway from last week's video teaching or discussion?

We are all headed to an eternal home. Heaven and Hell are real. The return of Jesus is also real. Any moment could be our last. The fact that we will meet Jesus in death or His return should revolutionize the way we see our daily lives.

Pray that your daily lives would be changed by the reality of eternal life and the return of Christ.

WATCH

Use the space below to take notes as you watch the video for Week 5.

DISCUSS

Greg said, "If we believe that Jesus is coming back and it doesn't affect us and the way that we live, we have missed the point." What did he mean by missing the point?

What does the phrase "Memento mori" mean? Why is this not a depressing or morbid expression? How is it great news for believers in Jesus? How is it terrible news for non-believers?

What are the only two possibilities for how everyone's life on earth will end? What are the only two possibilities for how everyone will spend eternity?

What things are you glad to know will not last forever?

Read 1 John 3:3. What hope is John referring to?

How is faith in Jesus about abundant life now and eternal life forever? How are the two related? How are they distinct? What happens if we only focus on one or the other?

Read Luke 12:36–40. How should the wedding imagery shape our view of the future?

What was your biggest takeaway from Jesus' parable?

How was it a timely reminder?

WRAP UP

Use the following to wrap up your time together.

Would you be able to honestly say what D. L. Moody said about not changing anything if you knew that Jesus would return today? If not, what would you change about how you spend your time?

Knowing that Jesus will return, consider these takeaways:

1. How can we shine light in dark places? What opportunities have you had to be a witness for Jesus in the places you identified during Week 2's lesson on the Holy Spirit? Who do you know that isn't ready? How can you help them?

2. Are you ready to go? What does it look like to watch for Jesus, focusing your heart and mind on this great hope? How can it bring peace and joy even in uncertainty and darkness?

THIS WEEK

Time is your most precious commodity. How will you spend and invest it? With 100% certainty, you know that everyone will die—unless Jesus returns first. One of those two options will happen. Like you saw in Ecclesiastes (Day 2 of the first week's study), life is like a puff of smoke in the wind. Life is short.

If you believe God's Word is true, you believe that everyone will face judgment and an eternity in heaven or hell. This truth should revolutionize the way you live. Today could be your last. It could be anybody's last. It will be many people's last. You, along with everybody you know and the countless people that you don't know, will all stand before Jesus one day. Do you really believe that?

While people like to talk about heaven, it's understandable that they either avoid or get upset if the subject of judgment and of hell comes up in conversation. Nobody wants to think about judgment. They for sure don't want to think about hell as a possibility or even a probability. But when you see what the Bible says about judgment, heaven and hell, the gospel message of salvation through faith in Jesus truly becomes good news! This week, you'll read and reflect on what the Bible says about eternity. Be prepared to share something with your group from one of the following days:

DAY 1
Jesus and Eternity

DAY 2
In My Father's House

DAY 3
New Heaven and Earth

DAY 4
The Final Judgment

DAY 5
Personal Reflection

Day 1
JESUS AND ETERNITY

His master said to him, 'Well done, good and faithful
servant! You were faithful over a few things; I will put you
in charge of many things. Share your master's joy.'
MATTHEW 25:21

Most people who believe in some version of heaven also believe heaven will be a place of joy and reward. Who wouldn't like the idea of eternal happiness and blessing?

The problem is that too often, the gospel has become a ticket into heaven after you die rather than a message of God's will being done on earth as it is in heaven. When this happens, people begin to think of heaven like the world's greatest retirement plan—you make your investment here and there and reap the rewards later. Jesus certainly never gave people the option of "easy believism," meaning that if you just believe that certain facts are true, then you will go to heaven. Belief in Jesus is about more than walking an aisle or praying a prayer. Those things are not insignificant, but faith is demonstrated in the way we live.

What Jesus did teach was that heaven and hell, eternal joy and judgment, are as real as the ground beneath you right now. Life beyond death is not a separate reality disconnected from your life right now. What you believe about your future will shape how you live in the present. Your life before death affects your life after death.

Write John 3:16 in the space below, either from
memory or by copying it from your Bible.

This popular verse is clear about the reality of eternity. If you believe that everyone will either perish or live eternally, it should motivate certain behaviors and desires. Your belief about eternity should change the way you pray for and interact with other people. All people are loved by God and facing eternity with Him or apart from Him; they will either perish or live—forever.

**What word or phrase would you use to summarize each
of the following parables of Jesus from Matthew 25?**

☐ **The Ten Virgins (Matthew 25:1–13)**

☐ **The Talents (Matthew 25:14–30)**

☐ **The Sheep and the Goats (Matthew 25:31–46)**

You may have come up with a variety of words or phrases to summarize Jesus' teaching on life and the kingdom of heaven, but His vivid imagery makes clear that we should live in anticipation of His return, making the most of what He's given to us, and loving others as He would. You should live eager to hear Jesus tell you "well done, good and faithful servant" (Matt. 25:23).

**What does the life of a "good and faithful
servant" look like today?**

You have a mission. You've been entrusted with a great responsibility. You have the truth about the kingdom of heaven. You can either help see more and more people join the kingdom of heaven, or you can hide the gospel in fear, worried that you might somehow do something wrong. Romans 1:16 says the gospel has the power to save, not the gospel messenger. Your job is to simply spread the good news of Jesus. The only way you can truly mess that up is by not sharing at all.

> **To end, read and reflect on Matthew 7:21–23.**
> **Pray that your belief in the gospel will motivate you to**
> **share and show the love of Jesus to people around you.**

Day 2
IN MY FATHER'S HOUSE

In my Father's house are many rooms; if not, I would have told you. I am going away to prepare a place for you. If I go away and prepare a place for you, I will come again and take you to myself, so that where I am you may be also.

JOHN 14:2–3

Certain English translations of the Greek language in the verses above led to the misconception that we'd all have "mansions" in heaven. A popular TV show, The Good Place, recently played with this idea. Anyone whose score for good things added up to outweigh the bad things they did in life went to the good place instead of the bad place after dying. Everyone in the so-called good place had a dream home to fit his or her personality and preference.

But the better translation is "rooms." In Jesus' time, much like if you were to visit Israel today, it would be common to see homes under construction with new additions being built onto an existing house. When a young man was engaged to be married, he would leave his bride-to-be for an unknown period of time in order to prepare a place for them to begin their new life together as part of his family. When the father decided that everything was ready, he would send the son back for his bride (remember yesterday's parable of the virgins?). This is why Jesus could say to His disciples that even He did not know exactly when life as we currently know it would come to an end and the kingdom of God would be more fully established (Matt. 24:36 and Acts 1:7).

John 14:2–3 is less about what you get and more about what Jesus will do. What promise did Jesus make?

On a scale of 1–10 (1 = never, 10 = constantly) how often do you think about Jesus' literal return?

Related to the common belief in our culture addressed in Day 1 (that if an afterlife exists, then it must be an existence of happiness and blessing, a reward for being a pretty good person in this life) is the misconception that everyone will be there—at least, everyone we'd want to be there would be. Again, who doesn't like the idea of heaven not only being an eternal retirement plan but one big happy family reunion or class reunion too?

Copy John 14:6 into the space below.

According to Jesus's teaching in John 3:16 and John 14:6, who will experience eternal life with the heavenly Father? How does this teaching differ from the way many think about heaven?

Jesus did "go away" for three days as He was crucified, buried, and raised from the dead, but 40 days after that, He returned to His heavenly Father's presence. Two thousand years later, we are still eagerly anticipating His return. It could truly come at any moment (Matt. 24:36–44). The question for you today is, are you living as if Jesus is preparing a place for you? How does the truth of God's Word shape your daily life?

What does Acts 1:1–11 reveal about Jesus leaving, His return, and what we are to do until that time?

To end, read and reflect on Colossians 3:1–3. Pray that you would eagerly anticipate Jesus' return, like a bride waits for her groom.

Day 3
NEW HEAVEN AND EARTH

*Then I saw a new heaven and a new earth; for the
first heaven and the first earth had passed away, and
the sea was no more. I also saw the holy city, the new
Jerusalem, coming down out of heaven from God,
prepared like a bride adorned for her husband.*
REVELATION 21:1-2

Perhaps the most popular picture of heaven is the cartoonish scene of an angel strumming a harp while sitting on a cloud. How many times have you seen death represented by a spirit floating out of a cartoon body and into the sky? While most of us would laugh at such childish depictions, knowing not to take them as serious theological expressions, we may also not have a much better description to offer for our eternal life after death.

**What does Revelation 21:1-3 reveal about our future
home with God? Do we go "up" to live with Him? Are
we disembodied spirits? Will we leave earth forever?**

What does Revelation 21:4-6 promise?

**Although the scene is clearly worshipful, how is
Revelation 21:22-22:5 different than turning into
an angel who plays a harp in the clouds?**

In the end—which is really just a new beginning—God will finally live among His people. All of Creation will be in perfect harmony with God and each other. Christ will make all things new, not all new things. We don't abandon this world when we die and fly away to the sweet by and by. Ultimately, God brings heaven and earth together, and His new city is established on earth. So, on the one hand, you will live forever in heaven, but you will also live forever on a redeemed earth. You don't go to heaven for eternity in a ghostlike spiritual state to be with God. He comes down from heaven to be with you as you live eternally in a renewed physical body on a renewed planet earth.

God's plan for humanity and the world didn't fail. He didn't throw away His original design and go back to the drawing board after sin and death entered into Creation. The entire Bible tells the story of how God created all things in the beginning and is making all things new in the end. (Gen. 1–3 and Rev. 21–22.) His desire is to be with His people—forever.

What are you most looking forward to from this description of the new heaven and earth?

How does it change the way you think about your life now to see that eternity is not a completely different type of non-physical existence?

What does it reveal about God to see that from beginning to end His purpose has not changed for your life and for all of humanity?

To end, read and reflect on Revelation 22:20. Pray that your heart would eagerly desire for the Lord Jesus to come soon.

Day 4
THE FINAL JUDGMENT

Then I saw a great white throne and one seated on it. Earth and heaven fled from his presence, and no place was found for them
REVELATION 20:11

Did you know that the expression "All roads lead to God" is true? It is. But it's not true in the way people say that they believe that want it to be true.

All religions can't be true. All non-religious philosophies can't be true. Jesus clearly said that no one comes to the Father but through Him and that whoever believes in Him will not perish but have eternal life.

Either that's true, or it isn't.

C. S. Lewis famously said that Jesus could not possibly be considered a good moral teacher to be respected among other religious or philosophical figures in history. Based on statements like those in John 3:16 and John 14:6, He had to either be a liar, lunatic, or the Lord. His claims (and those of many other religions) simply aren't compatible with other belief systems as being equally true and valid. If any religion claims to be the only way to be right with God, which Christianity does because Jesus did, it's either true, or it isn't.

"All roads lead to God" because one day every person will stand before God Almighty. The Bible says, one day every knee will bow and every toungue will confess that Jesus Christ is Lord (Rom. 14:11). "All roads lead to God," but only one road leads to heaven.

Yesterday you looked at the new heaven and earth in Revelation 21–22. Today you'll also look at the lake of fire in Revelation 20–21.

Why do you think that most people are uncomfortable talking about hell and God's judgment?

What does Revelation 20:11-15 say about God's judgment? How does this fit with the teachings of Jesus that you've read on previous days this week?

According to Romans 1:18-23, how is God's judgment part of His good and holy character, not in conflict with it?

In his letter to the Romans, Paul wrote that all people are without excuse before God (1:20). Everyone is guilty. Only through faith in Christ can we be saved from ourselves and the wrath of God that our rebellion against our Creator and King rightfully deserves. (Jesus said the same thing in John 3:17–21.) Sin deserves judgment. Evil cannot be overlooked. God is just and holy. All who have experienced injustice will have peace. All who have acted wickedly will answer for their sin against God and one another. This is good and loving.

But in God's goodness, He not only judges evil, He also brings salvation. If a building is on fire, it's not unloving to tell someone that they need to change what they're doing, believe the truth about the situation, and follow you in order to live. There's no excuse to not believe. But there's also no excuse not to share.

Who do you know that needs to be saved from the path that they are currently on—one headed toward a final and eternal judgment? When will you tell them?

> **To end, read and reflect on Matthew 7:13–23. Pray for endurance and discernment in walking the narrow path and in helping others along the way.**

Day 5
PERSONAL REFLECTION

Use this space to reflect on everything you've been reading this week about eternity.

What specific truths or general ideas have been meaningful to you?

_____

_____

_____

_____

_____

_____

_____

_____

_____

_____

_____

_____

_____

_____

Week 6

WHAT CAN WE DO NOW?

START

Begin with a quick review and time of sharing. Be mindful of how God is at work in your life.

What is something that you learned or experienced in a new way during last week's reading?

What was your biggest takeaway from last week's video teaching or discussion?

In this final video, we'll see that the Great Commission is not only a commanded mission for our obedience but also a great blessing for our happiness. We join the revolution Jesus started with His own disciples by living in joyful obedience to proclaim the gospel and make disciples.

Pray that Christ would begin a revolution in your own hearts that would be undeniably attractive to the world around you.

WATCH

Use the space below to take notes as you watch the video for Week 6.

DISCUSS

In closing, Greg mentioned that younger believers need older believers to help stabilize them, and older believers need younger believers to help energize them. How have you experienced this in your own life?

What is a foundational truth that you have "rediscovered" when teaching them to a child, a new believer, or even in discussion during this study?

Read Matthew 28:18-20. Why is believing in Jesus the starting line, not the finish line for the Christian life?

How does "making disciples" include what we typically think of as "evangelism" and "discipleship"?

How did Greg's definition of evangelism as "building a bridge" help remove some of the common fears or misconceptions about evangelism?

What are some practical ways to build bridges with people who don't yet believe the gospel? What are some ways to burn bridges?

Once someone crosses the bridge of faith, how can we help them continue to follow Jesus?

How does Jesus' declaration of having all authority and promise to always be with us give confidence and excitement for joining His work in the world?

WRAP UP

Use the following to wrap up your time together.

Whom did God use to reach you with the good news of His salvation? Whom has God reached through you in evangelism?

When did you first experience the joy of salvation in Christ? What was the most significant change in your life? How did you feel? What would it be like to help someone else experience those feelings and changes?

What has been your biggest takeaway during this study of Jesus Revolution?

How have you experienced the Spirit working in and through you in new or refreshing ways?

THIS WEEK

This is not the end! Hopefully, it's just the beginning of an exciting new perspective on your life, the world around you, and eternal realities! Your six-week journey is coming around full circle to see how God has been at work, preparing you for what's next.

Nobody knows when the Spirit will bring the next great awakening or revival, but you do know the things that people do when He moves.

This week, you'll read and reflect on what the Bible says about new life in Christ. Even if your group is not meeting again after this last video session, don't skip this final week of personal study—it's what everything has been building toward over the last six weeks. Each day has an incredibly powerful and practical tool to help equip you for joining God's work in the world.

If your group is meeting again, be prepared to share something with your group from one of the following days:

DAY 1
Jesus and the Prodigal Son

DAY 2
The Harvest is Ready for Workers

DAY 3
Be Ready to Share Good News

DAY 4
Discipleship and the Church

DAY 5
Personal Reflection

JESUS AND THE PRODIGAL SON

*But we had to celebrate and rejoice, because this brother of
yours was dead and is alive again; he was lost and is found.*
LUKE 15:32

In one of the Bible's most moving stories, Jesus uses the relationship
between a father and his two sons to illustrate the nature of salvation. Before
the parable of the lost son, two shorter parables about the lost sheep and the
lost coin contain previews or spoilers as to Jesus' main point.

**What is the invitation at the end of both
parables in Luke 15:1–10?**

Summarize each character's story from Luke 15:11–31.

Younger son

Father

Older son

What hope did Jesus offer?

What warning did Jesus offer?

How did you rebel against God or take His love for granted?

What happened to bring you to your senses?

**When did you go from lost to found,
from spiritually dead to alive?**

**How have you experienced the lavish
grace of your heavenly Father?**

Remember Jesus' purpose in telling these parables according to Luke 15:1–3. Even though the tax collectors and sinners were listening too, Jesus directed these stories at the Pharisees and scribes who were complaining that He associated with these so-called "lost" people like the younger brother.

The family of God has no entitled "sons" who look down upon a brother (or sister) as being less deserving of love, forgiveness, and the joy of being part of the family. We have a Father who sees us even when we are far off and runs toward us, full of compassion, in order to celebrate in His joy over our salvation.

> **To end, read and reflect on Isaiah 12:4. Pray that out of an overflow of the Father's joy for your salvation, you would join Him in seeking lost brothers and sisters so that they, too, can experience the joy of His love.**

Day 2
THE HARVEST IS READY FOR WORKERS

Then he said to his disciples, "The harvest
is abundant, but the workers are few."
MATTHEW 9:37

Jesus often used natural imagery in His teaching and parables. He likely gestured to nearby scenes as He taught on grassy hillsides, along dusty paths, or near the water's edge. Even if they weren't immediately visible, the mental pictures are clear even when reading His words two thousand years later in our own American context.

How did Jesus describe people in Matthew 9:36?
What did He mean?

What did Jesus tell His disciples to do in Matthew 9:37–38?
What do you think that meant?

Use the following to identify your own harvest fields.

Where do you spend most of your time?

Write as many names as you can think of within that harvest field.

Where are you around the most lost people?

Write as many names as you can think
of within that harvest field.

Who are your neighbors and family members?

Write as many names as you can think
of within that harvest field.

Go back into each of your harvest fields and circle
the names of Christians who you can pray will join
the work of evangelism and discipleship.

Put stars next to at least one person in each
field that you will pray for their salvation.

To end, read and reflect on Romans 10:8–15.
Pray for more workers and for a great harvest.

Day 3
BE READY TO SHARE GOOD NEWS

In your hearts regard Christ the Lord as holy, ready at any time to give a defense to anyone who asks you for a reason for the hope that is in you.
1 PETER 3:15

Peter was just one disciple whose life was forever changed by Jesus. Related to the opening verse, he was the first to identify Jesus as the promised Savior and Son of God, but he then quickly stuck his foot in his mouth by trying to tell Jesus how to be the Messiah (Matt. 16:22). Later, Peter was caught off guard before the crucifixion and denied knowing even Jesus three times (Matt. 26:69-75). After Jesus' resurrection, Peter not only preached the first sermon (Acts 2:14-40) but was constantly being questioned and challenged by the same religious leaders who had Jesus executed and regularly imprisoned or beat Peter (Acts 3–5).

> **What does 1 Peter 3:16 say about the attitude we should have toward people who don't know Christ yet?**

The Apostle Paul went from a great persecutor of the church to one of the greatest missionaries. Look at what he wrote to a young man he was mentoring.

> **In 2 Timothy 4:1, what reason does Paul give for what he's about to say in the next verses?**

Copy 2 Timothy 4:2–5 into the space below,
underlining all of the action verbs that Timothy
is personally responsible for doing.

To help you be "ready at any time," use the following space
to think about and write out a simple gospel presentation.
Verses have been provided if you need them.

What is God's desire for people (Luke 19:10; John 3:16)?

What is our great problem as people (Romans 3:23)?

What did Jesus do to make a relationship with
God possible again (1 Corinthians 15:3-4)?

How must we respond to Jesus (Romans 10:9-11)?

How does this give us a renewed perspective
and purpose in life (Romans 12:1-2)?

To end, read and reflect on 2 Corinthians 5:18–20. Pray for opportunities
to share the gospel and to see people reconciled to God.

Day 4
DISCIPLESHIP AND THE CHURCH

Jesus came near and said to them, "All authority has been given to me in heaven and on earth. Go, therefore, and make disciples of all nations, baptizing them in the name of the Father and of the Son and of the Holy Spirit, teaching them to observe everything I have commanded you. And remember, I am with you always, to the end of the age."
MATTHEW 28:18–20

In the Great Commission, we have answers to all six of the key questions about what the Jesus Revolution is and how we're to be a part of it.

1. WHY: "All authority." The purpose of Jesus' life, death, resurrection, ascension, and future return isn't just so that we can believe that it's true and go to heaven when we die. He started a revolution and invites us to join it right now, today. Ultimately, because it's His mission, it can't fail.

2. WHERE: "Go." Wherever you go and while you are going, be intentional to join Jesus in His mission. He may or may not call you to go to a faraway place or for a long period of time, but God always wants you to live with intentionality.

3. WHAT: "Make disciples." Don't just be saved, be a good person, etc. Your job as a disciple of Jesus is to make more disciples of Jesus. A disciple is someone who is learning how to be like someone else, not just learning about or learning from them. Your life should look more and more like Jesus' life as you help others grow more and more into Christlikeness too.

4. WHO: "All nations." For God so loved the world. This will mean going out of your way, getting uncomfortable, getting over prejudices or preconceptions or preferences. Jesus was constantly crossing geographic, ethnic, social, political, cultural, and religious borders so that all people can experience the kingdom and will of God, our Father.

5. HOW: "Baptizing" and "teaching them to observe." This means the Christian life of the Jesus Revolution is related to the church. Baptism has always been a symbolic but sacred act that identified a person with new life in Christ and new life with the community of His people, the church. God himself exists in relationship (Father, Son, and Holy Spirit). There's no such thing in the Bible as a Christian who loves Jesus but not the church. Churches aren't perfect and so we need one another for everyone to continue growing in Christlikeness. This happens as we all learn to live out the truth of God's word. Faith is not just head knowledge to be believed, but wisdom to be observed and lived out in practice. That's true faith.

6. WHEN: "Always, to the end of the age." Following Jesus starts with a decision, but it's more than just a one-and-done deal. The Christian life is an every day, every moment dying to yourself and living for Jesus. This doesn't happen in your own strength. He is with you and empowers you in this new life.

What do we learn about following Jesus from the great commission?

How will you live out the great commission in your life?

> To end, read and reflect on John 17:17–21. Pray for personal commitment to a local church community and to the mission of Jesus. Pray for church unity, health, awakening, and revival.

Day 5
PERSONAL REFLECTION

Use this space to reflect on everything you've been reading this week about your life with Christ.

**What specific truths or general ideas
have been meaningful to you?**

WHERE TO GO FROM HERE

We hope you were challenged and inspired by *Jesus Revolution*. Now that you've completed this study, here are a few possible directions you can go for your next one. See more at LifeWay.com/BalancedDiscipleship

SHARE
CHRIST

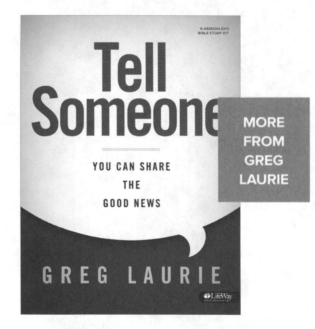

TELL SOMEONE
You Can Share the Good News
Greg Laurie

Discover the simple joy of evangelism as the good news of Jesus naturally overflows into your daily life. (6 sessions)

Leader Kit $49.99
Bible Study Book $14.99

LIVE UNASHAMED

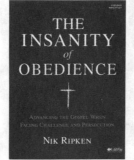

THE INSANITY OF OBEDIENCE
Advancing the Gospel When Facing Challenge and Persecution
Nik Ripken

Help your group learn to walk with God in tough places and follow Jesus joyfully, even in persecution. (6 sessions)

Leader Kit $49.99
Bible Study Book $14.99

SERVE GOD AND OTHERS

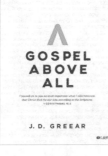

GOSPEL ABOVE ALL
J.D. Greear

Discover that the impetus for the church's ministry is not a new strategy or an updated message but a return to elevating the gospel above all. (8 sessions)

Leader Kit $99.99
Bible Study Book $14.99

LIVE UNASHAMED

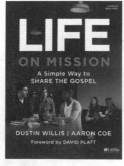

LIFE ON MISSION
A Simple Way to Share the Gospel
Dustin Willis and Aaron Coe

Learn how to live a missional lifestyle from prominent pastors and authors who live it themselves. (5 sessions)

Bible Study Book $10.99

ORDER ONLINE OR CALL 800.458.2772.
Prices and availability subject to change without notice.

MORE FROM
GROUPS
MINISTRY

DIFFERENCE MAKERS
How to Live a Life of Impact and Purpose
Gregg Matte

Get off the sidelines of ministry and let Jesus work through you as you pray, go, and give of yourself to make an eternal difference. (6 sessions)

Bible Study Book $14.99

LifeWay.com/DifferenceMakers

SOMETHING NEEDS TO CHANGE
A Call to Make Your Life Count in a World of Urgent Need
David Platt

Be inspired to respond to spiritual and physical needs with urgency and Christlike compassion. (8 sessions)

Leader Kit $79.99
Bible Study Book $14.99

LifeWay.com/SomethingNeedstoChange

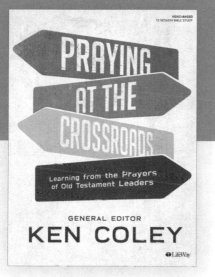

PRAYING AT THE CROSSROADS
Learning from the Prayers of Old Testament Leaders

Ken Coley, General Editor

Study the ancient prayers of Old Testament leaders at critical moments in their faith journeys. (12 sessions)

Leader Kit $99.99
Bible Study Book $14.99

LifeWay.com/AtTheCrossroads

COUNTER CULTURE

David Platt

See how the gospel compels followers of Christ to counter culture on a wide variety of social issues in the world around them. (6 sessions)

Leader Kit $99.99
Bible Study Book $14.99

LifeWay.com/CounterCulture

ORDER ONLINE OR CALL 800.458.2772.

Prices and availability subject to change without notice.